The Pig Dance Dreams

part III of **The Black Barns Trilogy**

I — *Rediscovered Sheep* (Brick Books, 1989)
II — *The Bad Philosophy of Good Cows* (Black Moss Press, 1989)
III — *The Pig Dance Dreams* (Black Moss Press, 1991)

The Pig Dance Dreams

John B. Lee

Black Moss Press

© 1991 by John B. Lee

This work was completed with the aid of a Works in Progress
grant from the Ontario Arts Council.

Some of the poems herein first appeared
in the following publications:
*Black Apple, Carousel, Small Worlds, Broken Glass, Fossils of the Twentieth Century,
Quarry, Poetry Canada Review.*
"The Pig Farmer's Wife"
was read on The Radio Show (CBC).

Published by Black Moss Press, P.O. Box 143, Station A,
Windsor, Ontario, Canada N9A 6L7.

Black Moss books are distributed in Canada and the
United States by Firefly Books Ltd., 250 Sparks Ave.,
Willowdale, Ontario, Canada M2H 2S4.

Financial assistance toward publication
was gratefully received from the Canada Council
and the Ontario Arts Council.

Typesetting and page design by Kristina Russelo.
Cover art by Juan Villaneuva Luna.

Canadian Cataloguing in Publication Data

Lee, John B., 1951-
The pig dance dreams

Poems.
ISBN 0-88753-221-7

I. Title.

PS8573.E348P44 1991   C811'.54   C90-090463-1
PR9199.3.L33P44 1991

for my mother and sister

Contents

Shouting Who We Are	8
Photograph: My Sons and the Hog-Yard Pigs	10
What Will it Buy Me this Coin of the Heart	11
Pig Dentistry	13
The Nutting	15
Ringing Sows	16
Loading Pigs	18
Pretend You Are Happy	19
The Cold Event	20
Runts	21
Mending Gate	22
Dunnville Pig Races	24
The Better Self	26
The Corpselessness of Memory	27
When I was in High School	28
The Heart on the Cutting Board	30
Formaldehyde	31
How Sigmund Freud Gets Puzzled Interpreting the Dreams of Rural Folk	32
Garnet is Gone	34
Rondeau of a Swineherd	36
Those Damned Confederation Poets	37
The Swill Pail	39
Cleaning Out Hogs ii	40
Stickless	41
To Find and Forgive	42
The Killing Bees	43
The Connection	46
There's lots of them Ma and Pa butchers in the country now	47

The Slaughterhouse Field	54
Translations From a Death	55
On the Way Home From the Meat Factory I Decided to Be a Poet	56
Anthony-Pig Favoured by Little Girls	58
Piglets	59
Rachel and the Little Pigs	60
Eating the Young	62
No Silk Purse, But —	64
Certain Creatures There Are	65
Rhinitis	66
He Has Those Big-Thing Blues	67
Brian Keeps Pigs	68
Arnold Ziffle	69
Guinea Pigs in the Hayloft: a Tale of Lost Virginity	70
Our Shadows Cross Again	72
The Pig Farmer's Wife	73
Poem for the Man who, Dressed All in Feathers	74
Pig Roast	75
The Train Wreck	76
Swine Into Water	77
"The Boats Were Used to Carry Pigs"	79
The Pig Mirage: an Elegy	81
The Pig Dance Dreams	83
Pig Angels	85
Bay of Pigs — Photograph of my Father Vacationing in Cuba	86
Pigs	87
The Hogs of the Sixties	92
Blind Pigs	93
A Game of Pig	95

Shouting Who We Are

After chores
the inconsequential continent
of my father's discarded clothes
dusts the cold shed floor.

Hog-smell perfumed
with the talc of chop
puffed into the sleeves from leaning on the hopper
caught in the fine sift of their hunger
pigs nudge his boots from the trough rungs
and skid through a scarf of straw
circling like someone setting a pocket watch 23 hours wrong
then collapsing where he walks
rubbed from knee to cuff
by their hock-tinged paradigms of dung
and the bristled fabric of their hams
they race
breathe wet-snouted into the stuff he's left behind
their tongues powdered like an unlicked chalk gutter.

One miffed porker crabs the door
so it kicks on its hinges
while 5 cylindered noses
make a pink daisy chain ☉☉☉☉☉
in the chink of light
between the door-bottom and the cement stoop.

Not a lawyer
who hangs his weskit on a chair
loosens his tie, and stagily rolls up his sleeves
to address a jury.
Not a doctor
who wears his stethoscope
like a sacred necklace
touching the cold amulet to your heart.

Not a poet
bangled and rapt
buying the death of each brief moment
with the coins of his eyes
and the coin of his word.
Not a mortician
with the slow sad droop of his hands
draining from each stiff white cuff
like something frozen while it flowed.

But a farmer
up from the barn
unafraid of his nakedness
the shower raining in the little gutters of his flesh
swirls in the drain mouth
milky with what it has meant
to live this day
as we all live with it
shouting who we are.

Photograph: My Sons and the Hog-Yard Pigs

The hog-yard pigs pose
graphed by fence wire
and framed by railway ties
in the hog yard beside the scalding house
where my uncle dug in the ancestral tell
and found an old embrocation bottle
once filled with horse liniment
the name welted on the clear glass
a message from the distant past,
how the acres took their toll
on a working joint
but the ghost of geldings
have set their forehead stars
in the midst of multitudes
and shrugged the harness from their withers
like a puzzlement of apple branches.

So, these pigs too,
cheese cut by the grid of fence
from snout, to poll, to ear tip, to jowl,
to hock, to tail —
Yorkshire, Landrace, Tamworth,
under the willow wisp
that hangs in the fall-blue heavens
like a heavy smoker's slender hand
and my two young boys
take the foreground with their smiles
dressed in coats
that haven't fit them for five years since,
I deny the falsification of time
with this 3 by 4 confirmation of smallness
and this only known existence of proof
outside of failing memory
of these particular pigs
their souls stolen
like bolt ends of widow's cloth.

What Will it Buy Me this Coin of the Heart

Those pigs that danced from my grandfather's chalk
from the simple blemished ⊙ of their snout
to the cursive flourish of their tail

knocked on the little blackboard
by the washroom door
like a game plan for life

his big man's arm
sweeping its mortal boom
upon the crude yesness of those days

when the sun was first-sex frantic
on the shag of grass
green as party ribbons
outside the window

and the sky was blue
as a brand new car

while uncle snorted chaff
in the sink
so it was whiskered with black nubs of hay
and the whole room was warmed with the smell of labour
when he opened the door.

But those pigs
are brushed
and the dust is clapped on brick
and the brick is washed with rain
and the rain
is tipped in the blushing soil
and the soil is faded by thirsty sky
and the sky is struck by thunder's hand
and the sun comes out like a lecher's coin

my heart has grown tight
as a fist around that precious offering

and what will it buy me
oh, what will it buy me
this ache
when the heart opens
and the palm is scored
with holding
the coin too long

and the coin moves in the world again
like the fatal commerce of seed
on the wind.

Pig Dentistry

My father picked up each piglet
tucked him under his arm
like a small watermelon
calmed the squirming
with the certain strategy of his strength.
The razor-sharp trotters
striking out from forelegs
scored his ample belly
with a red welt
like a surgical scar
healed over a missing organ.
My father grabbed these legs
running in air
stilled the surge when futility finally occurred
to the pink little thing
with radiant ears
the light shone through
ears like a bride's nightgown
in the bright bulb
that swayed like a hanged man on its cord
in the sty.

Then he took the wire cutters
from his hip pocket
and opened the pig's mouth
blunting the scream with the size of his hands
and the imperative of his pliers
went snip snip snip
sizing the black teeth
that would needle-prick the sow's teats
like a bad tattoo if they weren't taken
and I see them flying from the mouth
snip snip

like little wire ends they flew, making Gabby Hays
piglets, gummy at the back of their snouts
where they could have ripped your fingertip off
like the corner of a potato chip bag.

Then he sets them down
where after a moment's static revving
of their small hearts
they spin away
spitting out the remnants
of my father's dentistry.

ii

What would they have done
in the pre-domestic wilderness?

Made a horrifying shredded rag of her udder?
Pinkened her milk
like berries in breakfast cereal.

We live in such a humane society.
What would those of you who might call him cruel
have him do?
Lend his mind
to the prettifying makers of pork commercials.
Produce quirky little Disney movies
with all that damned big-eyed goodness
as if a boar could not tusk you open
so you spilled like wet groceries
from your own belly skin.

What would you have him do
for the sake of your delusions?
Starve you?

The Nutting

I look at the toothmark dimple
in my father's Kodiak boot
the tiny divot
in the blond leather
where the sow made her impression
her head cocked
her mouth snapping and frothing below his sock top
while he nutted her sons
and tossed their testicles in the straw
like a shaken plum tree.

My job is to hold the wriggling piglets still
while he slashes the scrotum
so the purpled cojones pop out
to be sliced free
but I can't take my mind off that sow
rushing in and out
like a grunting sumo wrestler
who dares once to bite my father's heel
then I jump the boards
crazed with fear.

My father merely clubs her snout with his elbow
and hurls another severed gland over his shoulder
so she turns to gobble the delicacy
distracted from her son's distress
by the prospects of deliciousness.

I crawl ashamedly over the partition
like foam boiling from beneath a pot lid
to spill my body beside my father,
one eye on the sow, one eye on the squirming piglet
gripped before the slash
and my third eye
turned inward
like a testicle lost in the straw.

Ringing Sows

When we weaned the shoats from their truffling dams
we had to ring the sows first
so they wouldn't root the yard.

Too much pain
before pleasure,
they'd be content
to take the flung-down chop,
the apple rot,
the swill, and unhusked corn we portioned out.

So my father would loop
a heavy rope
around the long-nosed landrace brutes
inside the upper jaw
where it caught on the teeth
as it would on the blade of a handsaw.

But she'd swing her head about
to bash the thing away
screaming and dragging her face
against the pen boards and the floor
till she gave up, panting,
or lost the tether
in a frothing storm
forcing us to start again.

Finally, if and when we had her
head-up against the partition
my father snapped the first sharp ring
in the flat flesh-disk of her snout
then another and another
each clamp we'd feel the surge
of her muscled flanks
along our trouser legs
till she was done
and jewelled
with the cheap utility
that kept her good-snouted
calm-nosed, reliable in the hog yard.

Loading Pigs

They'd run before us in the pen
like beads on a tipped flatboard
my father marking certain market-ready hogs
with a single red streak
along the bristled spine
got so's he could sight them
when they weighed ripe
the way a sculptor might pick a special stone
from the ordinary rabble.

Then we'd crowd the selected porkers
isolate them
circling
into the pocket of a corner
5 men
each with a flimsy plywood
nose-knocked and trotter scored
we'd shuttle them for the alley door
into the callejón
where they made their absurd corrida
leaping feed sacks
for a final exit through the trailer gate
or "Puerta de arrastre" (door of death).
Then they'd settle quietly oinking over the mile long road
like the conversations of retired school marms
on a rainbow-coloured tour bus
poking their curious noses at the passing landscape
as if they too expected to make a slide show
out of death.

Pretend You Are Happy

There's a pig riot in the brick barn
and my father goes down
with a cane
down to where those shoats
are taking out their grievances
on one poor weaner
whose side is streaked with toothmarks
his skin already red as a bad essay.
They're brawling
punks who won't quit
driving their jaws in his gut
and circling
while he pants half dead
weaving and stunned where they jam
his ribs like a slammed gate.

My father
goes in there
prying their jaws back
like a hammer clawing tough spikes
but he wins, being human,
and they, being pigs, lose.

What has this pig done?
It is the Lord's day, and everyone is pretending
they are happy —
everyone, that is, except pigs,
who have made their loud objections,
and children, bored with dull television
and the way the sun moves,
so slow every Sunday afternoon,
like a lazy bachelor looking for salt
in someone else's cupboard.

The Cold Event

I fell
through the mow-hole
into the hog's trough
that fit me
like a casket
measured out for children.

Into the slop
that porridged under the eating sow's nose,
into the mush
that splashed her oinking face
like a plaster maker's bad day.

And there I lay,
a grave digger's nightmare,
all angle
of arm hooked over the rim
tough-rooted to the shoulder
and my heart
pumping in the centre
like a bobbed-for apple,
and my brain blurry
as a voice talking under water,
the old sow looking at me
as if the mow-hole
had given birth, stepping away,
looking up as if she might expect
a twin.

Runts

My father
sends me into the sty
to kill runts.

I watch
the plump ones
nuzzling the sow for milk
feeding like carnivores
rending a recent kill
ramming her belly
with their hungry mouths.

Then
I look to the weak ones
congested, wobbly, angular with emaciation.
Their dry snouts
rooting impotently in the straw
their hunger real and undirected.

Never
robust myself as a child
never
did I suspect
that someone might have watched me
in the cradle
and wondered
if he should grab me by the leg
and beat me
against the door frame
thusly.

Make room
for the strong.
Make room
for the heinous urge
of immortality.

Mending Gate

for Robert Frost

Something there is that doesn't love a fence.
Pigs, for instance
will root cement slabs
from a mucky floor
to get at the world.
They'll worry the found interstices
the chinks
no bigger than a curlicue
will serve to prod their noses through.
They'll please
to heave at the slipshod gate
even as you watch
they'll snout-strike a gap
like convicts.
They'll dare their bulk against a wowing plank
the sow's gut plumping through the slats
till heave gives way
and the gate boards snap
into the garden
and then the pigs are free
flying along the squash rows
jowling down puddles of chomped tomato pulp
rasping beneath the greening trees
for windfalls
till one sow
roseated by the way a soft lawn
can be rutted like slop
makes for the edge of the corn field
which is where we found her
asserting her three dimensions
on a cob

snatched down and off
and when she sees us she
crashes into the corn rows
running between the stalks
into eighteen acres of crop
and we chase her back and up
across and down
the labyrinth until she's lost
in a fenceless realm
where pigs fall off the edge of the world.

When we leave her alone
to mend the shattered gate
she finds her way
back standing, waiting to return
to the world she knows
waiting as if to say,
"Good fences make good pigs."

Dunnville Pig Races

In mudcat days
at the mouth of the Grand
where it opens
like a drop-jawed sleeper
water lolls wasting a summer well
in willow shade
alive with a hundred hundred insects humming as one
like a happy girl doing the dishes
till her boyfriend comes
while every green moment grows greener
under the swoop of gulls
drifting like a flirt of ladies' evening gloves
in the blue over the swish of wind-washed trees
lightly tearing the shingles from the swell
to the very pools that hold a flagon's worth of shore silt
at the instep of tadpole-hunting boys.

Into this pitched like torches into oil
the pigs come wilding the crowd
toiling the muck with their trotters
pronged into the last rags of grass
clotting the air in their wake
squealing down the rattled gates
where every gambler's dance breaks loose
and tests a tall man's coffin's reach
or each loser rolls a swindled bill
and whispers with his hand
like the movement of a silk-sleeved dress
airing the melody of his girlfriend's arm
dreaming the cup of her breast

while a hampshire bangs his girdles
on the slats
or runs the slivered length
of a pen board with his pea-black eye
by the mob of snouts
racing in a chattered turbulence
like a wooden boat
snapped across the barrel of a jagged rock.

When all the humans have finally scuttled home
and the pigs are left
to grunt in the straw
after the young boar's loitered
and frothed till the last sow's dropped
her haunches
and saddled her jowls in her forelegs
snuffed once and gone to sleep,
then the river slowly loosens its grip on light
and tired sunset cards its crimson wool.

The Better Self

Bill canes the talced
pink-as-a-naked-librarian hog
so around he goes
in the show-ring circle
guiding the snout with a stick
hard like a vaudeville rouster.
Bill, with 15 other Bills
and 15 barrows
cracking those porkers like cops at a convention
and hating it all the while,
even these many years later
remembering how often we do what is expected of us
simply because it is expected...
not at all like those pigs
who bore against the cane
and screamed as if they knew
there is little wisdom in resistance,
but there is satisfaction,
and there is the memory of a better self.

The Corpselessness of Memory

Pigs can't sweat and
it was 5 days at the CNE show barn
upstairs
5 days with the thermometer reading 100 plus
then bursting
like an aneurism all red die
and throbbing apoplectic glass.

Piglets panting like lap dogs
sows lying importantly in clean straw
and shoats sluggishly checking their pens
then flopping
with their eyes open
desperate with torpor.
One ignorant swineherd
poured a pail of cold water
over a prize boar's back to cool him
but his heart exploded in his chest
and he lay dying like Jim Morrison
in an ice-cube bath in Paris,
but not half so romantic...

This hog
lay finally with all the symptoms of death
heavy as a small planet
his body a noiseless crowd of soft still organs
till he stiffened
like a Victorian church warden
and the heat wave broke
in the empty barn
5 days later
in the corpselessness of memory.

When I was in High School

Some said PIGS
were the easy bee-hive girls
with bouffant hair and mandrill face
breasts like candy cones in tight cashmere
that caught each lifted nipple like a licked gum drop
and skirts
that clamped the thighs in bondage.
And some said PIGS
were the uncouth futzing belching
ass-pinching jocks
with toothless grins like moonshine bootleggers
and all the vocabulary for vulgar sex
but none of the style.
And some said PIGS
were cops
gone bad and beating skulls
like home-run dreams
and flailing the grain of flower-children
till they broke on the threshing floor.
And some said PIGS
were presidents
and some said soldiers
and some said the rich
grunting in their coin under
splintered lamplight
fondling money-voiced Daisy Buchanan debutantes
tittering and vapid
while children starved
amidst the hot struggles of the poor.
And some said PIGS
were the establishment
whole governments, entire nations of swine,
one fabulously crooked sty from sea to shining sea.

But few said PIGS are US, few could admit to
the oink they'd made
though the oinking they'd made was loud,
a damned signature,
for either we're all PIGS under the skin
looking out or looking in
or we're one glorious masquerade
and the world wears us
to d/r/eceive the gods.

The Heart on the Cutting Board

The heart on the cutting board
and the heart on the desk
are pig's hearts
    pig's hearts
(oh my strange and weighty valentine)

The one is large, cold, sliceable.
The other — warm
from an electrocuted piglet
is removed from its wet casements
still throbbing
like the pink tip of a penis
making its final
palpitations in the black abyss of science.

Away from the entanglements of romance
I see life's raw red meat and
by slow insinuations
glimpse the incredible safety
of death.

Formaldehyde

In biology class
I take the tiny pig skull
between my slippery paws
my own head bent over
mouth parted in concentration...

for I have seen
the possibility of removing the brain
entire, intact, perfect,
a rippled cluster of white
floating and exquisite
like a drowned Ophelia.

Already I have peeled the flesh
and sliced the thin cranium
so it parts
a sliver
to reveal the delicate moonscape of intelligence.

I hold the tiny head in my palms
like a pomegranate
and applying pressure
my powerful hands climax
thumbs slipping
palm-heels punching egg-shell bone
pumping the brains
like sneezed porridge
splashing the inner dome of my mouth
then dropping
like wet plaster on my tongue.

I have tasted and spat out
the brutalized remains
the unforgettable cheesiness
the bitter, acrid pickle of defeat.

How Sigmund Freud Gets Puzzled
Interpreting the Dreams of Rural Folk

for Paul

The river of air
winding above the honey wagon
is befouled
beyond where the field lies
striped with the brown swathe
of liquid pig spoor.

Farm to farm, dogs drag their noses all afternoon
in the grass
and barn cats sneeze where they rest
in sun-drugged bunches
blinking and trying to sleep
the sleep of the beautiful.

Cars rush by
threaded with the glass-hugging stink
that weaves and settles and crawls
and sticks
like spider mites that flood the hand
that strikes the nest.

In the evening when a man lies
tuning his finicky bedside radio
the fetid breeze snakes the house
skimming brick
slides through the torpor
guillotined by a shuddering shut window
and then and there perfumes the pillowslips
and sheets and blankets rolled back
like sardine lids
invading pyjama collar and cuff
like a fragrant mistress.

Later a whole village
falls asleep one by one
like feet slipping off mossy underwater stones
with heads struck a sudden black
their faces upturned
coins drifting down the fathoms
of uneventful night.

They dream the noisome piggery
glancing in the mouth like a curled moustache
spilling in the brain
like a smoker's breath
and the stale remains of cheap cologne...
dreams that brown out
other possibilities
dreams that would trouble Freud
lost deep in the city
with neurotic women
and the gift of their urbane Viennese intellect
and their hogless fantasies.

Garnet is Gone

Without Garnet pigs will never be the same.

Old sows
like islands lifted from the water
and turned on edge
their fat hams
jiggling and white
the snapped rhubarb stink of their glands
the coelenterate wobble
in their jowls
the sloppy sack of their teats
swinging in rows
like a mob of unlit lantern wicks
the grand gossipy click
of their tongues
in dry chop
the gay snort they save for mud wallows
the way they suffer
the delirious boar's sniff
the mount and glide
of his curled priapus
they are steady and unshakeable
as a strong table you might stand on
to fix a light bulb

the barn partitions
thick with flies opiated by hog smell
and the sweet gluttony of swill
flies so slow you could swat a handful
like a scoop of buckwheat.

But with Garnet gone
his soul deep within the black water
of a night sky
the barn is as empty as the heavens
its half door
like the jaw hinge of a dead giant
creaks to an absence of hogs
so corporeal
you could carry it in the mind
like the sound of the wind
bracing a skin of ice to a dark and rattled branch.

Rondeau of a Swineherd

Pigs sniffling then snorting in dust of their chop
Rooting and sneezing like snuff takers in straw
They'd run, leap in circles, and then they would stop
To stare at whatever it was that they saw.

My father in workpants with twine for a draw
Banged the boards with his hands that made the chaff drop
Midst, froze for a moment before they would thaw,
Pigs sniffling then snorting in dust of their chop.

In dry corners sleeping so warmly they'd flop
And I'd bring them all humped, dragged down with a claw
Their bedding shook free where they'd wake and then hop
Or rooting and sneezing like snuff takers in straw.

And I'd give too-close ones a kick in the jaw
So they'd race the pen while their trotters clip clop
On cement churned up for a game in the flaw
They'd run, leap in circles, and then they would stop.

But Tom, the man hired to muck out their slop,
Hated mostly those pigs, which stuck in his craw.
He'd slap out his fork with a soft side-tined fop
If they dared stare at what it was that they saw.

Those Damned Confederation Poets

The pigs glide
in the slickened floor
roulette
the hopper
like bullets
thumbed one by one from a spun cold chamber.

I've seen them there
playing at the chase
with the flimsy to and fro
of Tom the hired man
busy with their stringy leavings
rushing so his boot tops
wibble-wobble their orange hoops
loose noosing his calves
till they wear a reddish welt
in the flesh
like a tea-kettle burn.

I've seen pigs slide
like ball players stealing a base
then bunch, then run again,
then jump, hover, then slide
like field beans in a swivelled sieve
gather into small gruntings
bump nose, or snout lift a belly
so it wiffles hock to ham
like a watery wine skin
or sneeze in the quick-limed floor
so their truffling nostrils vomit
dampish breathy decisions
in the new straw.

Then when they settle clean nested
their ears flip to shake away
the nursing flies
and they turn their intelligence to sleep.

Then Tom could sit in his chair
smoke and curse their hide
while his rolled trouser cuffs
stiffened like stretching cats
and every muscle
pumped its black-hearted ache
with his brain
policing the hurt of boot movement
in each blistered toe.

In his simple dream
he garottes pigs one by one
with binder twine
or plunges his four manure tines
till the pink skin
is pimpled with wounds.

So much for the romance of work.
So much for those damned Confederation poets
who would have made
farmers of us all.

The Swill Pail

It was a milk pail once
clean and bright
as the helmet of Athene.

Now it sits in the shed
beneath the sweat smell of Tom's chore smock
beside his buckled winter boots
the soles wickered with dry manure.

It lingers there for a half-week
taking the table scraps
(potato peels, half-eaten apples, and scrummed turnip
leavings)
forging a stew
a cold stinking chaos
a broth for the pigs.

My mother takes and hurls the swampy blend
so it arcs the fence
in a mottled rainbow
then she rattles the cloche of the empty pail
a clarion call for the hogs

who run tawoomping from corn-dreams
and the crib-rats lift their whiskered nares
to wiggle and sniff the wind
turning a golden kernel in their greedy little hands
like an expensive pocket watch.

Cleaning Out Hogs ii

Tom trundles
across the hog pen

his fork heavy with manure
dangling over tines

Tom dead
two years now
ten years since he did this job
sty empty, mow quiet
save the pigeons
that coo their soft slow percolating coos
and walk the fat safe tightrope
of beam and rafters.
Barn like a ghost ship
riding blue air
conjures even the carpenter's warm hands
where in the skeleton he sits straddled
with the blacksmithed nails still wet
and half-driven in the plank
fixed 'tween gravity and floating
in the strength of shoulder
forearm and cupped palm.

A dropped hammer stumbles
down the tumbling thumblength of a dream
set in time
like a smoker's single exhalation
dissipating in the street.

Stickless

"Speak softly, and carry a big stick."
Theodore Roosevelt, 1901

The old boar could smell fear
in a human
like fire in a rag
so his legs poured to a gallop
his trotters clicking their engines
intent on surgery of the tusks
to try a man's flesh
to test his cosmic tailor
by the zipperload

but Tom always
carried a sawed-off
hockey stick
for that boar, he'd come frothing
across the grass
at any man stupid enough to go
stickless

but he learned
to give Tom room.
The small thunder of a koho cracking
across his snout
rattled his tusks
and buzzed his teeth to the very roots
once too often.

So he learned
a man with a stick
is a man to be reckoned with.
A man with a stick
is a man
not to be contradicted.

To Find and Forgive

Poor Tom the hired man
left a little sickle-mooned gash
in the side of a pig
so it parted and closed
like a quietly dying philosopher's mouth
when the hog moved
around the pen.

Made his rage worthless
wielding the little chop shovel
like a backwoods preacher's Good Book
till he struck
once, left the deep fatal disfigurement
thus he culled her like a ruined daughter
and all the regret in his world wouldn't seal
the sorry gilt.

And the night blames the day
for parting with such ease
and the heart darkens like a smothered flame
and we enter the house of our selves
like chore-worn farmers
and every hour pregnant with death
we sleep off the little pulse kicks
of our own passing
where we might find and forgive
the water in the bottomless well of the soul.

The Killing Bees

i

My great-grandfather John gave the Indians
the sow's ears.
He gave them the snout
soft and round
like a morel.

They came to help
at the killing bee
pigs hooked and hung
like a rack of dinner jackets
the guts spilling in heavy loops
livid and steaming anacondas.

They would camp
in the orchard behind the sweet corn
where my grandfather
would have played with their children
when he too was a boy.

Sometimes when grampa John was in the mood
he would give them
the pig's feet
and a single ham
and their jubilation
would drift down upon his stoic farm.

ii

After the war
when the Indians still came to the killing bee
and helped carve up half a dozen hogs
so they hung
like pulpy wind chimes
from the apple boughs
and when the business
of lard rendering, hair burning, blood boiling
was done
and the whole was carbonadoed
like the parts of some soft uninventable machine
after the screams
had dried in the hills like a dishwasher's hands
and the hams wrapped in cloth
drooped in their nets
like a cookie maker's hair
then came the time to be generous
the best time for the division of heads
when the sun fell in the west
like a king's reason
and the clouds scraped their cutting-board horizons
in dull-knifed light of dusk
and even the wildest children
slowed at their play
like something kicking after it was hanged
then grandfather John
handed out the gift of hog's heads
one for each man
wrapped in a grain sack
and cinched with twine
but thinking like schoolboys doubled over
their arithmetic they stayed
till one stepped forward
cleared his throat like a slate of miscalculations
and spoke —

————— 44 —————

"John, since we been to war,
we got used to eating
a little further back on the pig."
and the other men nodded
so great grandfather reached up
and unhooked a half a dozen roasts
that hung like lanterns in the branches
and that seemed to satisfy — but it was the last time
the Indians ever came to the killing bee.

The Connection

We hang the hog from a lynching tree
for being what he is
hooks through hocks
and squirming.

Above him apples dream bad dreams
tucked in spring blossoms
with the terrible possibility of life.

The leaves shake
like a kitchen knife slow strutting the slats
of venetian blinds.

And the hog, wild-eyed
spills his blood by bucketsful
like a clumsy housepainter
while his voice
a gargled scream
slows to silence.

I am but a boy
and cannot manage the connection
between this event
and Easter Sunday dinner's
sweet pineapple ham.

There's lots of them Ma and Pa butchers in the country now

i

My uncle, Red Hocks John
with hair like a sunset squinnied at
through a swath of orchard grass
got to rambulating again.
This time he was on about
"ma and pa butchers,"
talking of them over a cup of tea
cooling like a sleeper's fever
in his palm
and black as tobacco spit.

They came to the farm and I imagine them —
man, wife, and son,
piling out of the car,
spilling their legs so their soft-soled shoes
baled the gravel like a shell purse,
the woman skipping sheep droppings
as she came.

"Vant lamb. Beeg lamb. Buck lamb."
This was papa
with hands rolling and coining the air.
I imagine the woman — tiny, with black hair
netted up like alfalfa sprouts
and her son
pasty as a cream dipper leaned
after it's drained the skimmings and left the curd.
"Vat you got? Lambs?"
"Yeah, we got lambs, hogs, a few cattle."
"You got peeg? You got boar?"
"Yeah."
"You sell?"
"Maybe."

"So I took them to the barn," Uncle John said,
"'nd showed them this one
whose nuts was ruptured. We should've cut him,
I guess, but we hadn't bothered.
So pa says, 'Not beeg enough.'
'Jesus H. Christ,' I says, he must a weighed 300 pounds.
'No, me vant beeger,' he says
so I took him out to see the old boar.
He was in the shed under the straw stack
and I kicked that old sow jumper in the pills
to get him up, cause I know'd there'd a been
no way to move him if I started off gentle.
Well he woomped out of there
like a chimney fire through a flue hole.
The old woman, she rucked up her skirts
and clumb the baler carriage.
Pa, he toed himself on the wagon hitch on the H tractor
barked his shin on the power drive
and danced into the seat
flappin' his arms like a guinea cock,
and junior cleared the gate
in one swoop. I still don't know how he done 'er,
peering through the slats from t'other side,
holdin' on so the whole shebang quivered
like a buggy-whipped lap dog."

"'Him not safe,' pa says.
'Him try to kill vife,' he says
his voice shakin' like he was ridin' a wagon wrack
across cow ruts and field stones.
'Nah, he's safe as yer mother's rockin' chair,'
I says, 'nd scratched him behind the ear
so he stood
takin' his pleasure in the sun.
'Me no vant. Him kill vife. Him vild boar.'
And they wouldn't come down
till I drove him away long enough
'nd far enough for his stink to cool."

At that Red Hocks John took a sip of his tea
swished his mouth, swallowed
and poured himself another bitter cup
black as beetle chitin.

ii

Uncle John starts in again
rocking back on his blond maple-wood kitchen chair
so the spools and spindles creak
like linen closet crickets under the story.
"I took them back the lane, after that,
to where the lambs was pastured.
'How about that one,' I says
pointing down to where one lay
saw-jawin' his cud
like Sammy Davis singin' Candy Man.
'Not beeg enough. Me vant beeg lamb.'
So I grabbed one by the chops wool.
He had knackers big as store-bought butternut squash,
a tail dock raggy with dung cots,
'nd hind legs a little turned out
and sickled — the kind of ram
you'd a kept in a root cellar
with the rutabagas
even if he was your only son and heir.
Well ma, she got busy pattin' his withers
thumpin' his rack,
and gettin' to know his nut-heft,
then when she nodded
old pa says, 'Ve'll take. Kill by car in yard, no?'"

"Strung him up like a horse thief
right from that there apple bough,"
John says pointing over his shoulder
at the apple tree just outside the dooryard fence.
"She put salt in a can so the blood
wouldn't curd when she slit the throat
and caught it in that, then she put it
in an old pop bottle — filled up one of them there
big plastic pepsis from the implement shed.
Took everything but the bleat, the penis and the stomach
turnings.
She even stripped the gut
for sausage casings.
Course I kept the hide.
'If you want to kill here,' I says,
'I get the hide.'
What the hell you'd do with a sheep pancreas,
I don't know," John says
conjuring it in his hands
like a mud wallop.

iii

"Why didn't they take the penis?" I asked.
John just shrugged like somebody was trying
to saddle him
with a starch-collared shirt.
"Saw a man take a bull penis, once,"
he said.
"Must a been six or seven feet long.
Spiked it to the barn.
Let it dry,
so's it got hard as a sulky shaft.
Made himself a whip out of it.
Bone-hard, it was.
Cut through the air
like a cavalry sword
'nd snap a pretty good welt
on the windy side of a market sow, too."
He laughed
and sipped enough black tea
to lighten the cup
then let the dregs seep back
and gather their money
like frog spoor.

iv

"Did they take the boar?" I asked.
"Hell no!" he said.
"I wouldn't a sold him.
He had a few good years in 'im yet.
I sent 'em back to Windsor
with that lamb
spread out in the trunk
like something the wind scatter seeded
red as staghorn sumac fruit."

I imagine them departing in a spume of dust,
the lamb's half-digested gut hay
unclenching in the apple grass
and the shucked skin shagged
over the white pickets on the yard fence
the bottle flies nursing
the last beads of fat
from the hide.

v

There is passion in this story,
and out there now
where the dead lamb's bleat
hangs in the air like ball lightning
and out there
where the old boar
upsnorts the dust in breathy whirlwinds
beyond where the weeping willow sways
like the housedress hips of a woman
singing "Jimmy crack corn, but I don't care"
while she does the dishes
beyond the apple bough
where the lamb spilled
like a thumbnailed milkweed pod
beyond the barn
where pigeons mourn the death of flight
beyond the clouds
that hover and roll across blue heavens
like dog hair combed loose in tufts
and blown along the grass
beyond the beach-shell moon
the ghosts of this story
rig their gossamer webbing
like spiders
in the crown
of a turned-over hat.

The Slaughterhouse Field

Sweet smell
of
blood wind
in the slaughterhouse field.

Drums of gore
in the back of the little white building.
Offal looped like sunning snakes
the colour of undertongues.

Puddles lit with oily rainbows
in the dung-middle.

Animal screams climb air
like the shriek of fire in a wet log.

Here
where hearts crowd a bucket
like buttons in a button jar.

Translations From a Death

Beyond the slaughterhouse
the wind smelled of mortality
measured in heavy branches
that seesawed above the field
like drunken conductors
where creek water strategized its pebbled bed
ruttling in thin silver slivers
while each corn stalk shook its tambourine
like a narrow-hipped girl
learning the tune of summer.

All afternoon hogs were murdered
while the sun slept like a dragon on its shifting gold
and our slow wagon
swayed lazily above each tire rut
moving half empty
beneath crow shadows that flicked
like drugged eyelids on the air.

My heart
rides the troubled ship of my bones
in search of harbourage
not quite so human.
Not quite so frail.
Not quite so full of blame.

On the Way Home From the Meat Factory I Decided to Be a Poet

On the way home from the meat factory
I decided to be a poet!
Because sausages hung
like the long braids of Slavic girls.
Because the old herd bull
took the worm of the bullet
in his skull
and fell like a dynasty.
Because the hogs
caught death on electric floors
and jittering were dragged still warm
in their fit's-midst
to be halved like apricots
with their blue guts spilling
a circus-clown's nightmare on the floor.
Because their heads came severed
like hill fighters
for the deli.
Because the puré came oozing into plastic tubes
cinched and cut
cinched and cut in log-lengths of cold meat.
Because the cattle fell
like drunks in metal stocks
then were carbonadoed and hung to cure
in the time it would take
to light a cigarette in the wind.
Because blood spilled in the gutters
under the peeled beasts
and ran bubbling still hot
for the reservoir.
Because the chainsaws whined in bone
like a mosquito night

###57

and the bandsaw cut clean portions
marbled with fat.
Because I hunger.
Because the hand that cuts the meat
feeds the city.
Because I hunger
and am human
on the way home from the meat factory
I decided to be a poet.

Anthony-Pig Favoured by Little Girls

Not the old boar
frothing his tusk in apple rot
nor the sow grunting
under his brackets
like a parenthetic seizure
nor the nousty flumps
who oink their sleepy pleasure
in the corner of the sty
but the sweet
piggy-whidden
little white piggy-whidden
smallest of the veers
is the kind young girls
especially young city girls prefer.
This tantony-pig
they'd cuddle and mother
swaddled like a favourite doll
pig snout
protruding whiskered
from an Emily Dickinson bonnet
suckling a baby's bottle
so he quivers
between cocked trotters
and squeals when he's squeezed in the blanket's fissure
like a bagpipe lesson.

Piglets

Piglets tussle
and sneeze busily in new straw.
Rush and rustle
like communion crinolines.
Root with upended china-cup noses,
pink in the buttery light
with nipples like children.

Then they quiet to the newness.
Settle to sleep and breathe
like a lazy drizzle
falling on a cloth cap
under half-torn webs that weave
their agitated ghosts
mended as they are against the white-washed beams

inviting me to lean on my chin there too
in the pricked-up galaxies of straw.

Rachel and the Little Pigs

Rachel dreams of little pigs.
A little girl, she chatters on, her blond locks
ringed about her temples.
She loves them like dolls and flowers,
loves them like high-swinging in easy weather
the sun in her hair
the branch bobbing when her small body
comes true
in the scythe-blade motions of freedom and joy
these small pigs
innocent as lukewarm tubs
beneath the smiles of tongue-clucking mothers
who stir up the suds
so the water rocks and shines on porcelain.
But she fears the sows
whose shadows hang and darken the straw
like a witch's hair in moonlight
and the boars
who razor at the pen slats
with winding tusks
and grunt like wine-drunk bachelors
going off to bed alone.

And Pat remembers how a boar
once filled a barn —
a hand-high giant, like a horse
with feathered working hooves
plodding down
to dwarf the apple boughs
to harrow up circles
shaking in his yokes so the harness straps
loosely slap his withers
and fierce blue-bellied flies fuzz above the creek
their jaws wet with horse blood

while the big fellows rest
by stamping clods
and swashing their tails
like housewives brooming cats...
huge as these were the hogs of her childhood
looking up to where a spine
arced above her
a cloud-scraping bow, a stool for angels
to get at the stars.

And, "Is there such a thing as GIANT pigs?"
she asks me
now she's lost the size of childhood rhythms
when things
unrivered
in dusty rainbows above her head
and all the world was huge and terrible
shook up full
to make her tiny bed
where pigs
could be the sky.

Eating the Young

With her nose, sow humps her nest
clean, dry, warm
as the inside of a careful woman's purse
left beside her
where she sits, one hand across the leather.

The she flops
with a tired woomph of air
gently grunting as if asleep
to bring forth one, two, three —
then a final nose blinks, pausing
through the pink petals of her sex
like the tongue of a sassy girl...
four piglets to suckle
the fat-American democracy of her teats.
Four, only four
born to articulate her milky abundance
each a little lord or lady at a banquet table
heavy laden.

My father, ever the egalitarian pragmatist
takes 2 runts
from a half-ruined washboard lean matron
with a litter of 15
and offers them the bounty
of this plump mother
rich with sap
each nipple pearled with a tear of its own excess
her young already glutted
flung like wine skins in the heatlamp.

These feckless nurslings teeter
towards her and she lifts her head
sniffing their strangeness
like fire in the straw
then she rises in rage and murders them there
her jaw snapping shut on the little chucks
like a half-set trap too strong for the hands.
This done she settles to sleep
by their corpses bent and tipped
torn-eared and dead as the moon.

Her own young awakened by the curious noise
lift their full bellies and walk
to explore the puzzling luke-warm stillness
in heat-fading flesh
enough
they turn and nuzzle sow's udder and
half-bored by the taste
bang her gut with their snouts.

No Silk Purse, But —

A sow's ear is no silk purse, but —
when the sun shines through
it is the pink
of a cuticle above the half moon
and in the presence
of such beauty
I might incline to kiss the snout's tip
on the soft snuffing zero of her nose
where her nostrils
have bent to blow the dust
about a beam.

But she would surely nosh
my glorifying osculation
testing the fleshy jaw like a husk of corn
and split the visible
bit of flattering face
like a banker biting a phony coin.

I must be content simply to behold
the radiant oracular beauty
and hold the gypsy vision
in my heart awhile
like a flash of the kicked-up petticoats
of Klondike girls.

Certain Creatures There Are

The weaner
sticks his nose deep into the trough
and blows
playfully so the water bubbles
like a boy's milkshake

OOBLEOOBLEOOBLE
OOBLEOOBLEOOBLE

then he looks up at me
where I am grinning over the half door
something passing between us
something of the tease
something of childhood's undiminished mysteries.

Rhinitis

How can a germ
bend your nose like that, old sow,
deviated like the septum of a bad boxer
the veins of your eyes
like the frayed end
of an unlicked thread
you cobble in the pig yard
unsteady
as a little girl in her mother's high heels
the large flattening sickness
of your body
turned
like a carpenter's warped board.
Life leaves you,
easy as salt blown from an open palm
by summer's frail breath,
and we suffer
nature's weak student's indifference
to what passes from the world
while the days lengthen
like a tall man's shadow
approaching a lighted doorway.

He Has Those Big-Thing Blues

Boar shakes his nose like a busted thermos
when he's kicked off the cob.

He has those big-thing blues
his sex
always out and swashing for sows
like a cavalry sword.

he's a river
pushed into a puddle
by a footprint on the shore...
a dull axe
wedged in a wet log
by the idea of food
and Christ
he counts every kernel like a rosary bead
taken from the unhusked whole
as from the thigh of a dancer
in yellow-sequined tights and a white slit skirt.

His body proves there is a fence
investing its trump of strength
along each board
so the corner post leans and rights leans and rights
like a cop looking in a car window.

Like most of us
he has no great ideas
and there is little comfort in being himself.

Brian Keeps Pigs

The pigs are cordial
at Brian's toy farm
in his neat little witch's cottage of a barn.

A few fattening
in each pen —
their clean straw spread open
like expensive overcoats on a guestroom bed.

We hear them inside
before Brian enters and taps the slop-bucket bottom
conducting the noise
while one gilt
holds her high C
like a factory whistle over a ghostly
pre-dawn parking lot.

Then for a moment
they pause
looking up over the boards
into the sheen of his visage
like children gazing
into the beatific face of Christ
expecting the miracle of food.

Arnold Ziffle

Arnold Ziffle
breaks and runs naked
through the living room
as if he's embarrassed to have humans
for parents.

The only pig in the house
looking everywhere for an image
like somone desperate for a cigarette
or a poet
on a hockey team...

he needs to verify
what makes the sporty classes yawn,

but God is surely the kind of God
who will be curious about him too.

Guinea Pigs in the Hayloft: a Tale of Lost Virginity

How they studied
in the musty school of the hayloft
by the guinea-pig pens
in the priestly feel

lifting aside
the heavy gate of their youth
beneath
the intermittent choir of pigeons
mothering in the scattered dark

blemished with light
that bled
in shafts through nail wounds in the sheet
and marked the floor
as with a coin worn thin.

It was not love
that made them walk sockless
on the fish-spined floor's cool sift

the gentle tug of petals holding on
their dry lips
touched and parted
while each heart plunged like an unhooked rose
down down in
the little pink-bricked well
of their being.

They embraced and fell in the naked brush of green
their bodies entangled
like kite string
caught in the high black branches of their need.

It was not for love
but for the cleft that made her female
pressed in white silk
like a kiss in a kleenex
and for the stalk of his manhood that grew dangerous
and sticky as jam on a shirt cuff.

And he found her blunt thorn
and crafting a pearl in her wound
felt the faint flares of light
in the softly draining amazement of her eyes
like the slowly spreading stain of crushed berries.

No, they could not live
within the smoking contours of that day
when the snowless grass was furred with dusk
like a squirrel pelt
where they moved in their separate bodies for the light that
wept
from a far warm kitchen.

Our Shadows Cross Again

The Vietnamese pot-bellied pigs
grunt softly on "The Radio Show"
lift their toy snouts
and sniff the rags of air
winding about their nostrils
and lazily nosh their dusty tongues
as if to taste the light.

Again our shadows cross
like coffee voices.
Far from the wild thrashing in the undergrowth
under red flannel sunsets
they have grown faithful
lappable, they plot their lives
like ordinary dinner portions
scattered with a stingy gift of salt
long ago
forgetting it's best to live away from humans
beneath a dangerous moon
where breathing is more than breathing
and the heart makes necessary drumming
like something startled and reckless
locked in the jailcell of the ribs.

The Pig Farmer's Wife

The pig farmer's wife
has 300 pairs of elegant shoes.

They sit in her closet
till she selects one pair
then wobbles
out to the piggery on spiked heels
while the evening pumps
the sky with a billion stars
over the softish "sucketta sucketta"
of her stiletti in the muck
sour water brewing in the tiny wells,
the counter eruptions that populate
each wound
with a brimful uric liqueur
for the shiny beetledine.

So there she is trotting the manurey glebe
with her spare shoes
cloistered like nuns in the little shack
150 miles from the nearest town
the vogue of the sty
but those trim-foot hogs
only stare and grunt, "Umpf?
What's that to me? I wish for nothing more
than cob and slop.
Why she splatters out
for this dumb ballet
as if she could improve the beast
with rhinestone
and make a better heaven of her feet
than those two odd stars
I count by looking up.
I wish she would but scuttle the dance
and litter the yard with winesaps."

Poem for the Man who, Dressed All in Feathers,
Dove in a Vat of Pig Manure and Ate an Apple for $10,000

In this age
I have seen cows
line up at the manure spreader
for the dung delight
of hog excrement,
gather there and wait
for the fork to release its steamy burden
a delicacy for those cows
who'd fight for their delicious portions
swinging their horns
from side to side, woofing the competition
in the barrels, lifting a heifer while her hind cluts
stroked the air.
But we worked till the box was plumped up
from tractor tongue to beater bars
then it would pull away
leaving those disappointed bovines
mauling the tire marks
and snuffing big-nostriled at the half door
beyond which the pigs were promise-grunting
in fresh straw.

So perhaps it should come as no surprise
in this awful age,
when we fashion humiliations
and self-contempting freakishnesses
to read of someone disappearing beneath the murk
of liquid pig manure
to eat an apple for $10,000
in cold hard cash
or to hear in the clack of beater bars
applause for heroes
who name their own price for glory.

Pig Roast

The evening bends close
like a secret-telling girl
and the shadows
fit their form

while a suckling turns slow on the spit
and people move in the smell
on the perfumed hill
by the house above the embered pit.

The flesh is sleek on the hog
in the heat
and the door claps once and the door claps twice
on the porch next the pool
near the field at the road
where breeze is calm as a priest
who blows a candle out.

One voice rises above the low talk
talk low as the softly mothering cluck
of hens in the dark
the voice of a ghost broken
on the wheel of life
who hung her hurt self
like a coat in a closet
alone she mourns unheard in the beer
unheard in the drunken sway of a branch
unheard in the cutlery click and the clink of glass
unheard in the tired splash
of a single swimmer's arm
unheard in the gay sizzle
of fat in the fire
where the hog holds to the spike in his roasted mouth
like a single word sharpened
in the heart of his head.

The Train Wreck

Where the train cars
were lying
you could hear
the trapped pigs screaming.
Some of them were running loose
their sides torn
trailing guts
like glutted blue ribbons.
Some had shattered bone
thrashing in sockets of flesh
like swizzle sticks.
Some were spinous
with splintered slats
they'd ripped from the walls of the boxcars.
Some were grinding their ruined snouts
in the earth
or rubbling their busted haunches
against the embankment,
and some lay panting paralyzed
wild-eyed, frothing at the mouth
while local kids poked at their sides
as if they were prodding ant hills.
How they laughed
when the pig tried to move. .
How they resented
their scolding fathers
gathering them
moving them away.
How they longed
to climb into the dark cars
and look boldly
on the horror, the horror.

Swine Into Water

"suffer us to go away into the herd of swine"
Mark 5. 12.

There once were swine
  lazy grazing beside Galilee
    in the land of the Gadarenes
      during the time of radiance.

They were a large herd
appled on the grass
grunting and snuffling as pigs will
half-bored, their pink snouts
truffling and rooting
leaving their trotter marks in the glebe
like the cast of iron flowers
pulled downward from the roots
and left two-petalled in the aftersuck.

Their high song
fattened the air above the jittery tail-curl
and unconsecrated swine-stink safety.
Then Christ, who came upon an evil "legion"
inhabiting a beggar
who howled like a cave wind
where he lived
away from all humanity,
blessed and suffered these demons
to depart into the herd
apportioning each hog's head with one fiend
so the doomed peccary drowned his horror
in the dark water
black and smoking with demise.

"Behold"... the sublime sea
  embalmed and windless in the aftercalm
    emptying its cork of pig
      like the flotsam of a ship
        where it grinds its crop upon the strand.

"The Boats Were Used to Carry Pigs"

for Trudi Birger (after a story in the Toronto *Star*
Sunday, June 18, 1989)

May 5, 1945,
the day Germany surrendered
five days after Der Fuhrer
immolated himself and his bride
in the bunker
on Seelige-Adolfstrasse — "Beloved Adolf Street"
in the rubble of Berlin,
five days
after Magda Goebbels poisoned her precious kinder
in their sleep,
five days
after the agenslaga of the loyal Waffen SS
and the Wehrmacht that fell beside boys
like sun-scorched blooms
in their neighbourhoods,
five days
after the ubermensch, this "superman"
who seized upon "blood and soil"
this "philosopher of the future"
this "proud and brutal barbarian"
lay slumbering in his final imbecility
like wind-blown dust,
then the desperate "Germans"
who would "leave no trace"
carried in a boat meant for pigs
a few half-starved survivors
of the death camp Stutthof
intending to hurl them into the Baltic Sea.

Some thirty, mostly women and girls,
lean-ribbed as glue-factory horses
suffered one last indifference to their humanity
rocking like empty kegs crowded in the swine-hold.
But when the craft struck bottom
the crew clamoured,
knowing how perilous an evidence they carted,
"Throw the Jews into the water"
they might have said
as Nietzsche did
"the good old days are gone,
in Mozart they sang themselves out." So they sat inert
till all were saved,
lodged in the lapping sea
the dog-faithful, ever-lapping sea.

The Pig Mirage: an Elegy

for Dianne

In the dry Saskatchewan summer
the lake bed
quilted with fissures
broad and rainless
barren gaps split wide
where one hen ran crazy with thirst
till she fell
in the earth cracked open
to a dust-stuffed V
stuck and broken
like a grudge between brothers
her feathers clocked the days
without water
her unemployed bones cramped broken-necked
to a final mark in the crevice
like a hinge print in ash

and the heat pressed
its thin white palm
through the breathless choke of sky
arced and closed
like blue coffin satin
the night came
as an undertaker's jacket
thrown over the stars
with the stink of dry sweat
blown about the stridulating heavens.

Into this blasted mudless abscess
a single pig zig-zagging
desperate for drink
pivoted in the sore of his track
over every burnt inch
till his eyes caught
a greasy shimmering smear
where water made its last putrid sigh
in the cob-webbed throat of morning.

The farmers
found him there — drowned
his snout
like a smothered black rose
thrust
in the air
while crickets dragged their shrill
sharp
cruel fiddle sticks in the brain.

The sun
would make a tired slave
of every flower face
burning its baked petals
in the cockeyed light
like the cracked lips of a poor beast
starved for water.

The Pig Dance Dreams

The man who dreamed
a pig
dancing on his chest
leaving pronged trotter marks
in the flesh
dancing to wrestle
his jowl
against a human cheek
pig saliva sudsing
at his ear
dampening his hair so it clung
to the straw tick
wondered
if God loved him enough
to send this lean razorback.
Every night
he came like a lover
to grapple and wear the man out
dancing on his corduroy ribs
poking him in the belly
snorting at his nostrils
hot pig breath
winding like a fetid river
into his lungs
until he was startled awake
clawing up
from sleep like a bird
in a chimney flue
to find no pig
but his hands smelled of swine
and his ears were tender screams
of swine

and his arms were bristling
angry with spiked hair of swine
and his mouth
had the taste of raw swine
his tongue lathered
with his own mad speech
his own fear
pushed against his teeth
so they ached like the ribs of a cage
holding in some
live animal with the urge to rend
explode a prayer
along his jaw
"God! Take away this pig."
so he fell
into pigless sleep
tame sleep lucid sleep with no room
for darkness
just a thin light always on
docile and cold as a fridge light
when you opencloseopencloseopenclose
the large white door.

Pig Angels

Pig angels are wingless
though they fly like noisy arguments
in a bad marriage.
Pig angels sit
on the right hand of ... whatever ...
each a fat indifference ... a bricolage ...
Pig angels walk
like someone crossing a hot beach.
Pig angels sing their glories
like wine-drunk husbands
making love too fast on a rainy Saturday mattress.
Pig angels truffle
for draff
slow-snuffing the dust as if they sniffed
a former man in every particle
or bubble their buffeting snouts
in hogswallow for the drowned core
of things,
but when they land they land
like a thousand thousand birthday balloons
that have come unstuck from an archway
heavy with breath, touching
like the exquisite friction of familiar lovers
and every ordinary face
is eclipsed with coloured soul rainbows
and though life till then may have been
a dull nightclub comedian
listening in the wings to the grumbling meanness
of a fractious crowd
now the human hears
the miracle, the wild applause of pig angels
refusing to heckle
what he was.

Bay of Pigs — Photograph of my Father Vacationing in Cuba

"The best pigs in Cuba,"
he says, "would have been culls
in Canada."

I have an image of the way
we used to break the skulls of runts
like flawed pottery
so the lucky brothers would grow fat
on sow's milk
in the dishonest oligarchy of the sty.

Here in my living room
father shows me photographs
of fields
with crooked rows of etiolated lettuce
lying like faded pom poms
in the scar of shallow furrows,
and in one picture
he is sitting in the shade
with a small green lizard on his pantleg
and I wonder
who will judge
the comfortable democracies
which measure out their money
like frugal shop girls buying cheap coffee.
Povery has little consequence for the rich,
charity is always tragic,
that the lean dog is always the meanest
after a meal
and in the Bay of Pigs
for once the swine recognized the pearls
and cast them back in the oyster killing sea.

Pigs

Pigs watch the farm boy
leaning on the window frame,

know he cannot yet
be imagining
his Spanish professor
running through the alleys
of a Colombian slum
pursued by a thief
with a pistol.

This is what it is
to have the point of view of pigs.
Looking at a boy
leaning in through your window
like a neighbour dropping by
for coffee and conversation.

He cannot yet be thinking of
the South American president's son
posing for a picture
with the yet to be slaughtered
newspaper publisher
his hand holding a corner
of the soon to be purloined cheque
meant for a hospital,
his smile
urging his brown cherubic corpulence
into a pig-snout oval,
his teeth enveloped in a puff of ochrous lips.

The farm boy
innocent and sow-thistle green
leaning in
so his chin rests
on the dust raised by our dance —
we snort,
then stop to stare
at
the monumental boy
the forever boy
the pale-pigmented boy
long before he would even imagine
Latin American children
burning in their shacks
like chickens.

He can't even dream yet.
One day he'll speak Spanish
in a library
with a young lady from Bolivia,
this terminal boy
with his unilingual tongue
as stupid as a flake of straw.

Or how could he ever dream
that one day he'll sit
over continental breakfast
at a London hotel
with South American service girls
as shy as weeds in wool
and sick for home...
While we look out through eyes
wrong coloured
knowing that Spanish literature
will change forever
his way of looking at pigs
muy borracho on fermented chop
looking up at a boy looking in through a window without glass
we pick his face, we gather it
in our piggish way
like a flower.
He is our sweet pre-literate innocent
unworldly as a warthog in a thicket
racing at us with his clapping hands
loading us like dancing girls
from a busted cabaret,

but we have memories of hog swallow
and apples as brown and soft
as a Mexican girl's breasts.

We see the swill slopped over the fence,
the corn cobs hurled
trailing white husk wings
and falling like shot birds
in bunches in our yard.
We remember being slopped
so hungry we'd race across the way
slavering and squealing
our tamed intelligence prisoner of his fame.

Oh yes, he was famous and lovely
swinging his shining pail
and calling us
pw-ig, pwig-pwig-pwig.

Sometimes he'd tease ... till we'd begged
grunting and oinking
like worship.
He won't leave us screaming on meathooks
or scorch our hair with a blowtorch.
No! He won't slit our throats.
Not this boy with the laughing eyes
retreating with his pail
swung shining like a strung-up saint.

In the night
in certain jungle villages
they gather the men
naked in shivering circles
their hands criss-crossed over their genitals.

This pigs can believe.

The children and women
listen from the shacks
to the bone cracks
and wince to hear the rifle shots
one by one
that bring silence to the hill poets.

This pigs understand,
but not the boy.
Not the 4H boy
leaning in the window.
Not the blue-eyed boy
who slowly vanishes into a future
leaving behind a manhole
through which we can see the sun
and trees
withering and shrinking
sucked backwards into what will be
as we pop one by one
into nothingness

patriots confessing
and being shot in the head
by fascists
who hoik on our corpses.
Who leave us in a scream of sun
until we see again.

The Hogs of the Sixties

for Pier Giorgio di Cicco

All of the hogs of the sixties are dead,
though they squealed once,
like beauty queens in a dressing room
with too much hair out of place.

Now we believe in the police again.
Applaud even the bad ones when they drub skulls
like piñatas
or blunt their rage till bones shatter
like taffy cracked on a desk.
We mostly expect corruption
elect it, hold it high on our shoulders,
wave its banners, shake its hand gladly,
gather in tight kukulos
to spit on the graves of our former selves.
Laugh at the fashion
and the naïvete of youth
denying our own adolescence
while the crows caw on both shoulders
like five-alarm fires.
Tip-toe past our thinking
let it sleep off the daylight
so we can do do do what we want
ignore the heresies of conscience and concern.

We were an orchestra tuning itself
for the long silence between numbers
the whole universe hushed
with even God afraid to cough
and this noise, this cacophony,
this crescendo of indifference,
this cat-gut scrambling over insipid strings,
is our song, our mid-life coda,
but then we always did make too much
of music didn't we?

Blind Pigs

At night when the stars came out
like sheeps' eyes in headlights
did we not go to the hole in the barn and drink
when we were as young as the moon
and felt the hot first flight of whisky
and fingered the empty glass
that monocled a dark patch of grass
through swimmy air
that tipped our feet
so we wagged at gravity and laughed
in weird directions.
Did we not swivel like slowing tops
while our heads drifted
pillowed on a field stone,
brained like the lazy flies
two horses had switched all afternoon.

I remember someone puking in a drum
and wishing he weren't himself
angled like a rack of pipes
his mind slow-voiced
and watering down the afterlength of every word.

And in the morning
when light lay splintered in the creek
like tweezered hair
with heart-thumped skull
like a dog fast-slamming a tick
and the fat mosquitoes
dropping on their blood-plumped bulbs
from forearms marbled with rollable bumps

and lying
full-length on the pig-fleshed earth
while the heat-ovened hills
and tall grass whip-cracked
at the eyelids, hard fluttering
like pinched butterflies.

That was when the days were set out silver serviced
and the clock sun-dripped in the summer leaves
like buttered toast
when we were new-pimpled and loudly right.
But now we pass under porridge-grey heavens
like ants on a leaf blown across a pond
unstunable
cutting dull-knifed
into each crow-throated, dog-ganged night.

A Game of Pig

(Pig is a simplified version of bridge in which the queen of clubs,
the seven of hearts, and the queen of spades respectively are the
three most powerful cards if and when hearts are trump.)

I had hoped that nothing would change
and that we could spend every stolen hour
as we wished,
a family, gathered around this small table.

My mother-in-law — the queen of clubs,
my father-in-law — the seven of hearts,
my wife — the queen of spades
and I the player
with the golden hand he never plays
fanned in my palm
the small multitude of card hearts fluttering with
possibility
like those of little girls at a strawberry social.

But we must surrender
what we have
accept the passing of the deal
watch
the cards fade
like washed-out party dresses
until we too
take our place in someone else's afternoon of luck
at some strange and distant table
our own face
that of a king or mustachioed jack
covered
by the slow turning of a spade.

The Author

John B. Lee was born and raised on a farm near the village of Highgate in Southwestern Ontario. He now lives in Brantford, Ontario with his wife Cathy and two young sons.

Lee's poems have appeared widely both in Canada and abroad. He was named Runner-Up in the 1987 People's Poetry Award for his book *Hired Hands*. In 1989 he was winner of First Place in the Nova Scotia Poetry Awards, and he received First Place in the Roundhouse Poetry Awards for both 1989 and 1990. He was also short-listed for the Charterhouse Poetry Award in London, England for 1990. He has three books forthcoming: *The Hockey Player Sonnets* from Penumbra Press, *When Shaving Seems Like Suicide* from Goose Lane Editions, and a book for children, *Dilly Wakeup And The Runaway Head*, from Black Moss Press. Lee is currently working on a collection of poems — *The Moon is Never Lonely* — and is putting the finishing touches on *Dark and Dirty*, a detective novel.

Books by John B. Lee

Poems Only a Dog Could Love, Applegarth Follies, 1976
Love Among the Tombstones, Dogwood Press, 1980
To Kill a White Dog, Brick Books, 1982
Fossils of the Twentieth Century, Vesta Publications, 1983
Broken Glass, League of Canadian Poets, 1983
Hired Hands, Brick Books, 1986
Small Worlds, Vesta Publications, 1986
The Day Jane Fonda Came to Guelph, Plowman Press, 1989
Rediscovered Sheep, Brick Books, 1989
The Bad Philosophy of Good Cows, Black Moss Press, 1989